Fun Stuff

Cupcakes

pil

Publications International, Ltd.

Recipe development on pages 4, 8, 10, 16, 18, 22, 24, 26, 32, 34, 42, 44, 48, 52, 58, 62, 64, 66, 68, 70, 82 and 112 by Ruth Siegel.

Photography on pages 5, 9, 11, 15, 17, 19, 23, 25, 27, 33, 35, 43, 45, 47, 49, 51, 53, 55, 59, 61, 63, 65, 67, 69, 71, 75, 83, 85, 99 and 113 by Laurie Proffitt Photography, Chicago.
Photographer: Laurie Proffitt
Photographer's Assistant: Chad Evans
Food Stylist: Carol Smoler
Assistant Food Stylist: Elaine Funk

Pictured on the front cover *(clockwise from top left):* Hedgehogs *(page 4),* Friendly Frogs *(page 58),* Dinocakes *(page 8)* and Panda Cupcakes *(page 16).*

Pictured on the jacket flaps: Sweet Snowmen *(page 44)* and S'More-Topped Cupcakes *(page 112).*

Pictured on the back cover *(left to right):* Hot Chocolate Cupcakes *(page 70),* Fishy Friends *(page 26)* and Chocolate Easter Baskets *(page 32).*

ISBN-13: 978-1-4127-9666-8
ISBN-10: 1-4127-9666-0

Library of Congress Control Number: 2009931599

Manufactured in China.

8 7 6 5 4 3 2 1

Microwave Cooking: Microwave ovens vary in wattage. Use the cooking times as guidelines and check for doneness before adding more time.

Publications International, Ltd.

Contents

Animal Planet

Hedgehogs

1 package (about 18 ounces) chocolate cake mix, plus ingredients to prepare mix
1 container (16 ounces) chocolate frosting
   Black jelly beans
   Small round white candies
   Black decorating gel
   Candy-coated licorice pieces

1. Preheat oven to 350°F. Place 22 standard (2-inch) silicone muffin cups on large baking sheet or line 22 standard (2½-inch) muffin cups with paper baking cups.

2. Prepare cake mix according to package directions. Spoon batter into prepared muffin cups, filling two-thirds full. Bake 18 to 22 minutes or until toothpick inserted into centers comes out clean. If using muffin pans, cool cupcakes in pans 10 minutes; remove to wire racks to cool completely.

3. Frost cupcakes. Cut jelly beans in half crosswise for noses. Arrange jelly bean halves and round candies on one side of each cupcake to create faces; add dot of decorating gel to each eye. Arrange licorice pieces around face and all over each cupcake.

Makes 22 cupcakes

Colorful Caterpillar Cupcakes

    1 package (about 18 ounces) vanilla cake mix
1¼ cups water
  3 eggs
⅓ cup vegetable oil
   Food coloring
   Buttercream Frosting (page 126) *or* 1 container (16 ounces) vanilla frosting
   Assorted candies, candy-coated chocolate pieces, red string licorice and lollipops
   Multi-colored gummy worms

1. Preheat oven to 350°F. Line 22 standard (2½-inch) muffin cups with paper baking cups.*

2. Beat cake mix, water, eggs and oil in large bowl with electric mixer at low speed 30 seconds. Beat at medium speed 2 minutes or until well blended. Divide batter between 5 bowls; tint each bowl with different color food coloring. Spoon batter into prepared muffin cups, filling two-thirds full.

3. Bake 18 to 22 minutes or until toothpick inserted into centers comes out clean. Cool cupcakes in pans 10 minutes; remove to wire racks to cool completely.

4. Prepare Buttercream Frosting. Set aside 2 cupcakes for caterpillar head.

5. Frost remaining cupcakes. Place 1 cupcake on its side towards one end of serving platter. Place second cupcake on its side next to first cupcake; arrange remaining cupcakes, alternating colors, in row to create body of caterpillar.

6. Frost 1 reserved cupcake; decorate with assorted candies, licorice and lollipops to create face and antennae. Place plain cupcake upright at front of cupcake row for head; top with face cupcake on its side. Cut gummy worms into small pieces; attach to caterpillar body with frosting to create legs.

Makes 22 cupcakes

Use white paper baking cups to best show colors of caterpillar.

Colorful Caterpillar Cupcakes

Dinocakes

1 package (about 18 ounces) chocolate fudge or devil's food cake mix, plus ingredients to prepare mix

44 long chewy chocolate candies (3×¼ inch), divided

10 to 15 small chewy chocolate candies

1 container (16 ounces) chocolate frosting

Candy sprinkles and decorating decors

1. Preheat oven to 350°F. Line 22 standard (2½-inch) muffin cups with paper baking cups.

2. Prepare cake mix according to package directions. Spoon batter into prepared muffin cups, filling two-thirds full. Bake 18 to 22 minutes or until toothpick inserted into centers comes out clean. Cool cupcakes in pans 10 minutes; remove to wire racks to cool completely.

3. Shape 22 long candies into dinosaur heads. (If candies are too stiff to bend, microwave on LOW (30%) for 6 to 8 seconds to soften.)

4. Cut about 1 inch from remaining 22 long candies with scissors; shape each into pointed tail. Make 4 to 5 small cuts along length of candies, being careful not to cut all the way through. Curve candies into tail shape. Press and flatten small candies into rectangles; cut rectangles into small triangles for dinosaur spikes.

5. Frost cupcakes. Press candy head and tail into opposite sides of each cupcake; arrange candy triangles in between. Decorate with sprinkles; press decors into dinosaur heads for eyes.

Makes 22 cupcakes

Little Lamb Cakes

    1 package (about 18 ounces) yellow cake mix, plus ingredients to prepare mix
    1 container (16 ounces) vanilla frosting
   15 large marshmallows
      Pink jelly beans or decorating candies
    1 package (10½ ounces) mini marshmallows
      Black string licorice
   44 mini chocolate chips

1. Preheat oven to 350°F. Line 22 standard (2½-inch) muffin cups with paper baking cups.

2. Prepare cake mix according to package directions. Spoon batter into prepared muffin cups, filling two-thirds full. Bake 18 to 22 minutes or until toothpick inserted into centers comes out clean. Cool cupcakes in pans 10 minutes; remove to wire racks to cool completely.

3. Frost cupcakes. Cut each large marshmallow crosswise into 3 pieces. Stretch pieces into oval shapes; arrange on cupcakes to create ears. Attach pink jelly bean to each ear with frosting.

4. Press mini marshmallows into frosting around edges of cupcakes. Cut jelly beans in half crosswise; cut licorice into ½-inch pieces. Arrange chocolate chips, jelly bean halves and licorice pieces on each cupcake to create faces.   *Makes 22 cupcakes*

Little Lamb Cakes

Miss Pinky the Pig Cupcakes

2 jars (10 ounces each) maraschino cherries, well drained
1 package (about 18 ounces) white cake mix *without* pudding in the mix
1 cup sour cream
½ cup vegetable oil
3 egg whites
¼ cup water
½ teaspoon almond extract
Red food coloring
1 container (16 ounces) cream cheese frosting
48 small gumdrops
White decorating icing, mini candy-coated chocolate pieces, mini chocolate chips and red sugar

1. Preheat oven to 350°F. Line 24 standard (2½-inch) muffin cups with paper baking cups. Spray 24 mini (1¾-inch) muffin cups with nonstick cooking spray. Pat cherries dry with paper towels. Place in food processor; process 4 to 5 seconds or until finely chopped.

2. Beat cake mix, sour cream, oil, egg whites, water and almond extract in large bowl with electric mixer at low speed about 1 minute or until blended. Beat at medium speed 1 to 2 minutes or until smooth. Stir in cherries.

3. Spoon 2 slightly rounded tablespoons batter into each standard muffin cup, filling about half full. (Cups will be slightly less full than normal.) Spoon remaining batter into prepared mini muffin cups, filling each about one-third full.

4. Bake standard cupcakes 14 to 18 minutes and mini cupcakes 7 to 9 minutes or until toothpick inserted into centers comes out clean. Cool cupcakes in pans 5 minutes; remove to wire racks to cool completely.

5. Add food coloring to frosting in small bowl, a few drops at a time, until desired shade of pink is reached. Frost standard cupcakes. Place mini cupcakes, upside down, off center of each standard cupcake. Frost mini cupcakes.

6. Place gumdrops between two layers of waxed paper. Flatten to ⅛-inch thickness with rolling pin; cut out triangles for ears. Use icing and chocolate pieces for eyes; create nose with chocolate chips and sugar.

Makes 24 cupcakes

Mini Mice

1 package (about 18 ounces) chocolate cake mix, plus ingredients to prepare mix
1 container (16 ounces) chocolate frosting
1 cup white frosting (optional)
   Small black and pink hard candies or decors
   Small fruit-flavored pastel candy wafers
   Black string licorice

1. Preheat oven to 350°F. Line 48 mini (1¾-inch) muffin cups with paper baking cups.

2. Prepare cake mix according to package directions. Spoon batter into prepared muffin cups, filling almost full. Bake about 12 minutes or until toothpick inserted into centers comes out clean. Cool cupcakes in pans 10 minutes; remove to wire racks to cool completely.

3. For brown mice, frost cupcakes with chocolate frosting; use knife or small spatula to pull up frosting and create fuzzy appearance. For speckled mice, frost cupcakes with white frosting; use toothpick to add streaks of chocolate frosting.

4. Arrange candies on one side of each cupcake to create eyes, nose and ears. Cut licorice into 3-inch lengths; press into opposite end of each cupcake to create tail.

Makes 48 mini cupcakes

 *Tip* Cupcakes can be baked in advance and frozen, undecorated, in an airtight container for up to three months. Defrost them at room temperature for several hours.

Mini Mice

Panda Cupcakes

1 package (about 18 ounces) yellow cake mix, plus ingredients to prepare mix
1 container (16 ounces) vanilla frosting
44 large chocolate nonpareil candies or chocolate discs*
44 small chocolate nonpareil candies
8 ounces semisweet chocolate, chopped *or* 1½ cups semisweet chocolate chips
44 white candy sprinkles or decors
22 red jelly beans

Chocolate discs are available at many gourmet, craft and baking supply stores.

1. Preheat oven to 350°F. Line 22 standard (2½-inch) muffin cups with paper baking cups.

2. Prepare cake mix according to package directions. Spoon batter into prepared muffin cups, filling two-thirds full. Bake 18 to 22 minutes or until toothpick inserted into centers comes out clean. Cool cupcakes in pans 10 minutes; remove to wire racks to cool completely.

3. Frost cupcakes. Arrange 2 chocolate discs on edge of each cupcake to create ears. Attach 1 nonpareil candy to each ear with frosting.

4. Place semisweet chocolate in small food storage bag. Microwave on HIGH about 1½ minutes or until chocolate is melted, kneading bag every 30 seconds. Cut small hole in corner of bag; pipe kidney shapes on cupcakes for eyes. Place candy sprinkle on each eye. Place jelly bean between eyes for nose; pipe mouth with melted chocolate.   *Makes 22 cupcakes*

Panda Cupcakes

Chocolate Moose

1 package (about 18 ounces) chocolate cake mix, plus ingredients to prepare mix
1 container (16 ounces) milk chocolate frosting
½ to ¾ cup vanilla frosting
1 package (12 ounces) semisweet chocolate chips
2 tablespoons shortening
   White round candies
   Small black candies
   Black decorating gel
   Pretzel twists

1. Preheat oven to 350°F. Line 22 standard (2½-inch) muffin cups with paper baking cups.

2. Prepare cake mix according to package directions. Spoon batter into prepared muffin cups, filling two-thirds full. Bake 18 to 22 minutes or until toothpick inserted into centers comes out clean. Cool cupcakes in pans 10 minutes; remove to wire racks to cool completely.

3. Combine chocolate frosting and ½ cup vanilla frosting in medium bowl until well blended. (Stir in additional vanilla frosting if lighter color is desired.) Frost cupcakes.

4. Place chocolate chips and shortening in medium microwavable bowl. Microwave on HIGH 1½ minutes or until chocolate is melted and mixture is smooth, stirring every 30 seconds. Place chocolate in pastry bag or small food storage bag with small corner cut off. Pipe chocolate mixture into shape of moose head on each cupcake as shown in photo; smooth chocolate with small spatula. (Chocolate may need to be reheated slightly if it becomes too stiff to pipe.)

5. Arrange candies on cupcakes to create eyes and noses; add dot of decorating gel or chocolate mixture to each eye. Break off small section of each pretzel twist to form antlers. Push ends of pretzels into top of cupcakes.
        Makes 22 cupcakes

Chocolate Moose

Butterfly Cupcakes

1 package (about 18 ounces) cake mix, any flavor, plus ingredients to prepare mix
1 container (16 ounces) vanilla frosting
   Blue and green food coloring
   Colored sugar
   Candy-coated chocolate pieces
   Red string licorice, cut into 4-inch pieces

1. Preheat oven to 350°F. Lightly spray 22 standard (2½-inch) muffin cups with nonstick cooking spray.

2. Prepare cake mix according to package directions. Spoon batter into prepared muffin cups, filling two-thirds full. Bake 18 to 22 minutes or until toothpick inserted into centers comes out clean. Cool cupcakes in pans 10 minutes; remove to wire racks to cool completely

3. Divide frosting between 2 small bowls. Add one color food coloring to each bowl, a few drops at a time, until desired shades of blue and green are reached.

4. Cut cupcakes in half vertically. Place halves together, cut sides out, to resemble butterfly wings. Frost cupcakes; decorate with colored sugar and chocolate pieces. Snip each end of licorice pieces for antennae; place in center of each cupcake.   *Makes 22 cupcakes*

Butterfly Cupcakes

Tasty Turtles

1 package (about 18 ounces) chocolate cake mix, plus ingredients to prepare mix
1½ packages (12 ounces each) small chewy chocolate candies
Green food coloring
1 container (16 ounces) vanilla frosting
Chocolate-covered raisins, chocolate chips or candy-coated chocolate pieces
White decorating decors

1. Preheat oven to 350°F. Line 22 standard (2½-inch) muffin cups with paper baking cups or spray with nonstick cooking spray.

2. Prepare cake mix according to package directions. Spoon batter into prepared muffin cups, filling two-thirds full. Bake 18 to 22 minutes or until toothpick inserted into centers comes out clean. Cool cupcakes in pans 10 minutes; remove to wire racks to cool completely.

3. For each turtle, cut 2 candies in half; flatten slightly and shape pieces into feet. Shape 1 candy into turtle head. (To soften candies for easier shaping, microwave on LOW (30%) 6 to 8 seconds.) Stretch 1 candy into long thin rope; cut into ½-inch pieces for tails.

4. Remove paper baking cups; cut off ½ inch from bottom of each cupcake. Add food coloring to frosting in medium bowl, a few drops at a time, until desired shade of green is reached. Frost cupcakes.

5. Press candy head and tail into opposite ends of each cupcake; press chocolate-covered raisins into frosting. Press decors into head for eyes. Arrange 4 candy feet around each turtle.

Makes 22 cupcakes

Tasty Turtles

Monkey A-Rounds

1 package (about 18 ounces) chocolate cake mix, plus ingredients to prepare mix
1 container (16 ounces) chocolate frosting
1 container (16 ounces) vanilla frosting
  Yellow food coloring
44 chocolate discs
  Small black jelly beans
  Black string licorice

1. Preheat oven to 350°F. Line 22 standard (2½-inch) muffin cups with paper baking cups.

2. Prepare cake mix according to package directions. Spoon batter into prepared muffin cups, filling two-thirds full. Bake 18 to 22 minutes or until toothpick inserted into centers comes out clean. Cool cupcakes in pans 10 minutes; remove to wire racks to cool completely.

3. Frost cupcakes with chocolate frosting. Place white frosting in small bowl. Add food coloring, a few drops at a time, until desired shade of yellow is reached. Transfer frosting to pastry bag or small food storage bag with small corner cut off.

4. Pipe circle of yellow frosting in center of each chocolate disc for ears. Cut jelly beans in half crosswise for eyes; cut licorice into smaller lengths for mouths and noses. Pipe yellow frosting into oval shape on each cupcake as shown in photo; arrange eyes just above oval and ears on either side of cupcake. Arrange licorice noses and mouths inside oval. Use toothpick or knife to pull up frosting at top of cupcake into hair (or use pastry bag with special tip to pipe hair).

Makes 22 cupcakes

Monkey A-Rounds

Fishy Friends

1 package (about 18 ounces) cake mix, any flavor, plus ingredients to prepare mix
1 container (16 ounces) vanilla frosting
Orange, purple and blue food coloring
Assorted color jelly candy fruit slices
Colored round gummy candies
White round candies
Black decorating gel

1. Preheat oven to 350°F. Line 22 standard (2½-inch) muffin cups with paper baking cups.

2. Prepare cake mix according to package directions. Spoon batter into prepared muffin cups, filling two-thirds full. Bake 18 to 22 minutes or until toothpick inserted into centers comes out clean. Cool cupcakes in pans 10 minutes; remove to wire racks to cool completely.

3. Divide frosting between 3 small bowls. Add food coloring, a few drops at a time, until desired shades are reached. Frost cupcakes.

4. Cut jelly candies into triangles for fins and tails. Arrange white candies and gummy candies at one end of each cupcake to create faces; add dot of decorating gel to each eye. Arrange jelly candy triangles on top and side of each cupcake.   *Makes 22 cupcakes*

Fishy Friends

Celebration Cupcakes

Chocolate Sweetheart Cupcakes

1 package (about 18 ounces) dark chocolate cake mix, plus ingredients to prepare mix
1 container (16 ounces) vanilla frosting
3 tablespoons seedless raspberry jam

1. Preheat oven to 350°F. Line 22 standard (2½-inch) muffin cups with paper baking cups.

2. Prepare cake mix according to package directions. Spoon batter into prepared muffin cups, filling two-thirds full. Bake 18 to 22 minutes or until toothpick inserted into centers comes out clean. Cool cupcakes in pans 10 minutes; remove to wire racks to cool completely.

3. Blend frosting and jam in medium bowl until smooth. Cut off rounded tops of cupcakes with serrated knife. Cut out heart shape from each cupcake top with mini cookie cutter; reserve cutouts, if desired.

4. Spread frosting mixture generously over cupcake bottoms, mounding slightly in center. Replace cupcake tops, pressing gently to fill hearts with frosting mixture.

Makes 22 cupcakes

Easy Easter Cupcakes

    1 package (about 18 ounces) yellow cake mix, plus ingredients to prepare mix
    1 container (16 ounces) vanilla frosting
      Green food coloring
   22 sugar-coated colored marshmallow chicks and/or rabbits
      Assorted white candies

1. Preheat oven to 350°F. Line 22 standard (2½-inch) muffin cups with paper baking cups.

2. Prepare cake mix according to package directions. Spoon batter into prepared muffin cups, filling two-thirds full. Bake 18 to 22 minutes or until toothpick inserted into centers comes out clean. Cool cupcakes in pans 10 minutes; remove to wire racks to cool completely.

3. Add frosting to food coloring in small bowl, a few drops at a time, until desired shade of green is reached. Frost cupcakes.

4. Trim marshmallow animals with scissors or knife to fit on cupcakes. Place 1 marshmallow on each cupcake. Decorate edges of cupcakes with white candies.   *Makes 22 cupcakes*

Tip For the best results when baking cupcakes, place the muffin pans as close to the center of the oven as possible. If you need to use two oven racks, rotate the pans from top to bottom and front to back halfway through the baking time.

Easy Easter Cupcakes

Chocolate Easter Baskets

1 package (about 18 ounces) chocolate cake mix, plus ingredients to prepare mix
22 long chewy chocolate candies (3×¼ inches)
Colored candy dots or decors (optional)
1 container (16 ounces) chocolate frosting
Edible Easter grass (see Note)
Candy-coated chocolate eggs, gumdrops or jelly beans

1. Preheat oven to 350°F. Line 22 standard (2½-inch) muffin cups with paper baking cups.

2. Prepare cake mix according to package directions. Spoon batter into prepared muffin cups, filling two-thirds full. Bake 18 to 22 minutes or until toothpick inserted into centers comes out clean. Cool cupcakes in pans 10 minutes; remove to wire racks to cool completely.

3. For each basket handle, microwave 1 chocolate candy on LOW (30%) 6 to 8 seconds to soften. Stretch or roll candy between hands until about 6 inches long. Bend candy into handle shape; pinch ends slightly to make them pointed. If desired, attach candy dots to handles with very small amount of frosting. Place handles on waxed paper until set.

4. Frost cupcakes. Arrange basket handles on cupcakes. Place small mound of grass in center of each cupcake; top with chocolate eggs or other candies. *Makes 22 cupcakes*

Note: Edible Easter grass can be found seasonally at some candy and specialty stores. If it is not available, substitute tinted coconut. To tint coconut, dilute a few drops of green food coloring with ½ teaspoon water in a large resealable food storage bag. Add 1 to 1½ cups flaked coconut, seal the bag and shake well until the coconut is evenly coated. For a deeper color, add additional diluted food coloring and shake again.

Chocolate Easter Baskets

Funny Bunnies

  1 cup all-purpose flour
  1 teaspoon baking powder
  1 teaspoon ground cinnamon
  ½ teaspoon salt
  ¼ teaspoon baking soda
    Pinch ground nutmeg
  1 cup sugar
  2 eggs, beaten
  ½ cup canola or vegetable oil
  1 teaspoon vanilla
  1½ cups grated carrots (about 3 medium)
  12 standard marshmallows
  1 container (16 ounces) cream cheese frosting, divided
    Pink food coloring
    Assorted pink and blue candies and decors
  24 mini marshmallows
  12 red chewy fruit candies

1. Preheat oven to 350°F. Line 12 standard (2½-inch) muffin cups with paper baking cups. Combine flour, baking powder, cinnamon, salt, baking soda and nutmeg in large bowl. Beat sugar, eggs, oil and vanilla in medium bowl until well blended. Add to flour mixture; mix well. Stir in carrots. Spoon into prepared muffin cups, filling about three-fourths full.

2. Bake about 24 minutes or until toothpick inserted into centers comes out clean. Cool cupcakes in pans 10 minutes; remove to wire racks to cool completely. Cut each standard marshmallow in half with scissors; stretch slices slightly into oblong shape to create ears.

3. Reserve ½ cup frosting in small bowl. Frost cupcakes with remaining frosting. Add food coloring to reserved frosting, a few drops at a time, until desired shade of pink is reached. Pipe or spread pink frosting down center of each marshmallow slice. Arrange marshmallow ears on each cupcake.

4. Arrange candies and decors on cupcakes to create faces. Press mini marshmallows to flatten; add to faces for cheeks. Microwave chewy candies on LOW (30%) 5 seconds or just until softened. Pinch center of candies to form bow ties; place on cupcakes.   *Makes 12 cupcakes*

Funny Bunnies

Graduation Party Cupcakes

 1 package (about 18 ounces) white cake mix
1¼ cups water
 ⅓ cup vegetable oil
 3 egg whites
   Food coloring
 1 container (16 ounces) vanilla frosting
22 chocolate squares
   Gummy candy strips
22 mini candy-coated chocolate pieces

1. Preheat oven to 325°F. Line 22 standard (2½-inch) muffin cups with paper baking cups.

2. Beat cake mix, water, oil and egg whites in large bowl with electric mixer at medium speed 2 minutes or until blended. (Batter will be slightly lumpy.) Add food coloring to match school colors. Pour batter into prepared muffin cups, filling two-thirds full.

3. Bake 17 to 20 minutes or until toothpick inserted into centers comes out clean. Cool cupcakes in pans 10 minutes; remove to wire racks to cool completely.

4. Add food coloring to frosting in small bowls, a few drops at a time, until desired shades of school colors are reached. Frost cupcakes.

5. Place chocolate square on top of each cupcake. Place small dab of frosting in center of squares; attach candy strips for tassel and chocolate piece for button.

Makes 22 cupcakes

Graduation Party Cupcakes

Surprise Package Cupcakes

  1 package (about 18 ounces) cake mix, any flavor, plus ingredients to prepare mix
    Food coloring
  1 container (16 ounces) vanilla frosting
  1 tube (4¼ ounces) white decorating icing
66 chewy fruit squares
    Colored decors

1. Preheat oven to 350°F. Spray 22 standard (2½-inch) muffin cups with nonstick cooking spray or line with paper baking cups.

2. Prepare cake mix according to package directions. Spoon batter into prepared muffin cups, filling two-thirds full. Bake 18 to 22 minutes or until toothpick inserted into centers comes out clean. Cool cupcakes in pans 10 minutes; remove to wire racks to cool completely.

3. Add food coloring to frosting in small bowl, a few drops at a time, until desired color is reached. Frost cupcakes.

4. Pipe ribbons on fruit squares with icing to resemble wrapped presents. Place 3 candy presents on each cupcake. Decorate with decors. *Makes 22 cupcakes*

Tip Use an ice cream scoop to fill the muffin cups with batter—it's quick, easy and helps keep the pan clean.

Surprise Package Cupcakes

Pumpkin Spice Cupcakes

$1\frac{1}{2}$ cups sugar
$\frac{3}{4}$ cup ($1\frac{1}{2}$ sticks) butter, softened
3 eggs
1 can (15 ounces) solid-pack pumpkin
1 cup buttermilk
3 cups all-purpose flour
1 tablespoon baking powder
2 teaspoons ground cinnamon
$1\frac{1}{2}$ teaspoons baking soda
$\frac{1}{2}$ teaspoon salt
$\frac{1}{4}$ teaspoon ground allspice
$\frac{1}{4}$ teaspoon ground nutmeg
$\frac{1}{8}$ teaspoon ground ginger
Maple Frosting (recipe follows)
Colored decors or sugar (optional)

1. Preheat oven to 350°F. Line 24 standard ($2\frac{1}{2}$-inch) muffin cups with paper baking cups. Beat sugar and butter in large bowl with electric mixer at medium speed 3 minutes or until light and fluffy. Add eggs, 1 at a time, beating well after each addition.

2. Combine pumpkin and buttermilk in medium bowl; mix well. Combine flour, baking powder, cinnamon, baking soda, salt, allspice, nutmeg and ginger in separate medium bowl. Alternately add flour mixture and pumpkin mixture to butter mixture, beating well after each addition. Spoon batter into prepared muffin cups, filling two-thirds full.

3. Bake 20 to 22 minutes or until toothpick inserted into centers comes out clean. Cool cupcakes in pans 15 minutes; remove to wire racks to cool completely.

4. Prepare Maple Frosting; pipe or spread over cupcakes. Sprinkle with decors or sugar, if desired. *Makes 24 cupcakes*

Maple Frosting: Beat $\frac{3}{4}$ cup ($1\frac{1}{2}$ sticks) softened butter in large bowl with electric mixer at medium speed until light and fluffy. Add 3 tablespoons maple syrup and $\frac{1}{2}$ teaspoon vanilla; beat until well blended. Gradually add $3\frac{1}{2}$ cups powdered sugar, beating until light and fluffy. Add 1 to 2 tablespoons milk, if necessary, to reach desired spreading consistency. Makes $2\frac{1}{2}$ cups.

Pumpkin Spice Cupcakes

Taffy Apple Cupcakes

1¾ cups all-purpose flour
1 teaspoon baking soda
1 teaspoon ground cinnamon
½ teaspoon salt
1 cup applesauce
¾ cup sugar
½ cup canola or vegetable oil
1 egg
1½ cups chopped roasted peanuts
20 wooden craft sticks
2 packages (14 ounces each) caramels
5 tablespoons milk

1. Preheat oven to 350°F. Spray 30 mini (1¾-inch) muffin cups with nonstick cooking spray or line with paper baking cups. Combine flour, baking soda, cinnamon and salt in medium bowl. Stir applesauce, sugar, oil and egg in large bowl until well blended. Add flour mixture; stir until blended. Spoon into prepared muffin cups, filling three-fourths full.

2. Bake about 16 minutes or until toothpick inserted into centers comes out clean. Cool in pans 10 minutes; remove to wire racks to cool completely.

3. Line baking sheet with waxed paper; spray with nonstick cooking spray. Place peanuts on plate or in shallow dish. Insert craft sticks into tops of 20 cupcakes. (Reserve remaining cupcakes for another use.)

4. Place unwrapped caramels and milk in large microwavable bowl; microwave on HIGH 2 to 3 minutes or until melted and smooth, stirring after each minute. Working with 1 cupcake at a time, hold cupcake over bowl and spoon caramel over cupcake, rotating stick until cupcake is completely coated. Immediately roll in peanuts to coat cupcake, pressing nuts lightly with fingertips to adhere to caramel. Stand cupcake (stick side up) on prepared baking sheet. Repeat with remaining cupcakes. (Caramel may need to be reheated briefly if it becomes too thick.) Let stand 20 minutes or until caramel is set.

Makes 30 mini cupcakes (20 with caramel and 10 plain)

Tip: For a quicker version, simply drizzle melted caramel over the cooled cupcakes and sprinkle with chopped peanuts.

Taffy Apple Cupcakes

Sweet Snowmen

1 package (about 18 ounces) vanilla cake mix, plus ingredients to prepare mix
1 container (16 ounces) vanilla frosting
22 standard marshmallows
1 package (7 ounces) flaked coconut
44 large black gumdrops
Mini orange candy-coated chocolate pieces
Mini chocolate chips
Round green gummy candies
Red pull-apart licorice twists

1. Preheat oven to 350°F. Line 22 standard (2½-inch) muffin cups with paper baking cups.

2. Prepare cake mix according to package directions. Spoon batter into prepared muffin cups, filling two-thirds full. Bake 18 to 22 minutes or until toothpick inserted into centers comes out clean. Cool cupcakes in pans 10 minutes; remove to wire racks to cool completely.

3. Frost cupcakes. Place 1 marshmallow on each cupcake for head, arranging slightly off center. Lightly press coconut into frosting around marshmallow.

4. For each hat, press 1 gumdrop on countertop or between hands to flatten into 2-inch circle. Attach second gumdrop, flat side down, to center of flattened gumdrop with dab of frosting.

5. Cut orange candies in half with sharp knife. Decorate snowmen with chocolate chips for eyes, orange candies for noses and gummy candies for buttons, attaching to cupcakes with frosting. Separate licorice twists into 2-string pieces; cut into 6- to 8-inch lengths and tie around bottom of marshmallows to create scarves. Attach hats to tops of marshmallows with frosting.

Makes 22 cupcakes

Sweet Snowmen

Cupcake Ornaments

1 package (about 18 ounces) yellow cake mix, plus ingredients to prepare mix
1 container (16 ounces) vanilla frosting
Sparkling sugar (optional)
Red string licorice
Green and red fruit roll-ups
Small shaped candies and mini candy-coated chocolate pieces
22 gumdrops

1. Preheat oven to 350°F. Line 22 standard (2½-inch) muffin cups with paper baking cups.

2. Prepare cake mix according to package directions. Spoon batter into prepared muffin cups, filling two-thirds full. Bake 18 to 22 minutes or until toothpick inserted into centers comes out clean. Cool cupcakes in pans 10 minutes; remove to wire racks to cool completely.

3. Frost cupcakes; sprinkle with sparkling sugar, if desired. Cut licorice into pieces to fit across cupcakes; cut fruit roll-ups into strips. Create patterns on ornaments with licorice, fruit roll-ups and candies.

4. Poke 2 holes in top of each gumdrop with toothpick. Cut licorice into 1½-inch lengths; press into holes to form loops. Press 1 gumdrop into top edge of each cupcake to resemble ornament hanger.

Makes 22 cupcakes

Cupcake Ornaments

Festive Chocolate Cupcakes

¾ cup all-purpose flour
½ cup unsweetened cocoa powder
1 teaspoon baking powder
½ teaspoon salt
½ cup (1 stick) butter, softened
1 cup plus 2 tablespoons granulated sugar
2 eggs
1 teaspoon vanilla
½ cup whole milk
1½ cups chocolate frosting
　Powdered sugar

1. Preheat oven to 350°F. Line 12 standard (2½-inch) muffin cups with paper baking cups.

2. Combine flour, cocoa, baking powder and salt in small bowl. Beat butter in large bowl with electric mixer at medium speed until creamy. Add sugar; beat 3 to 4 minutes. Add eggs, 1 at a time, beating well after each addition. Beat in vanilla. Add flour mixture alternately with milk, beginning and ending with flour mixture. Spoon batter into prepared muffin cups, filling about two-thirds full.

3. Bake about 20 minutes or until toothpick inserted into centers comes out clean. Cool cupcakes in pan 10 minutes; remove to wire rack to cool completely.

4. Microwave frosting in medium microwavable bowl on MEDIUM (50%) 30 seconds; stir. Microwave at additional 15-second intervals until frosting is melted. (Consistency will be thin.) Dip tops of cupcakes in melted frosting; return to wire rack to allow frosting to set. (Frosting may need to be reheated several times to maintain melted consistency.)

5. When frosting is set, place stencil gently over frosting. Sprinkle powdered sugar over cupcake; carefully remove stencil. *Makes 12 cupcakes*

Tip: Stencils can be found at craft stores and baking supply stores. You can also make your own stencils by cutting out shapes from paper.

Festive Chocolate Cupcakes

Princess Power

Fairy Tale Cupcakes

1 package (about 18 ounces) cake mix, any flavor, plus ingredients to prepare mix
1 container (16 ounces) vanilla frosting
Pink, purple , blue and yellow food coloring
Silver dragees
Assorted decoratifs and decors

1. Preheat oven to 350°F. Line 22 standard (2½-inch) muffin cups with paper baking cups or spray with nonstick cooking spray.

2. Prepare cake mix according to package directions. Spoon batter into prepared muffin cups, filling two-thirds full. Bake 18 to 22 minutes or until toothpick inserted into centers comes out clean. Cool cupcakes in pans 10 minutes; remove to wire racks to cool completely.

3. Divide frosting between 4 bowls; add different food coloring to each bowl, a few drops at a time, until desired shades are reached. Frost cupcakes with pink, purple and blue frosting; smooth tops with small spatula.

4. Spoon yellow frosting into pastry bag with round decorating tip or small food storage bag with small corner cut off. Pipe crowns and wands on cupcakes; decorate with dragees, decoratifs and decors.

Makes 22 cupcakes

Fairy Tale Cupcakes

Marshmallow Delights

  2 cups all-purpose flour
  1 teaspoon baking soda
  1 teaspoon baking powder
  ½ teaspoon salt
  ½ cup sour cream
  ½ cup milk
  1 teaspoon vanilla
  1 cup granulated sugar
  ½ cup (1 stick) butter, softened
  2 eggs
    Green food coloring
1½ cups vanilla frosting
  3 cups fruit-flavored mini marshmallows
    Green sparkling sugar

1. Preheat oven to 350°F. Line 12 standard (2½-inch) muffin cups with paper baking cups. Sift flour, baking soda, baking powder and salt into medium bowl. Combine sour cream, milk and vanilla in small bowl until well blended.

2. Beat granulated sugar and butter in large bowl with electric mixer at medium speed 2 minutes or until fluffy. Add eggs, 1 at a time, beating well after each addition. Add flour mixture alternately with sour cream mixture, beginning and ending with flour mixture, beating well after each addition. Spoon batter evenly into prepared muffin cups.

3. Bake 21 to 23 minutes or until toothpick inserted into centers comes out clean. Cool cupcakes in pan 5 minutes; remove to wire rack to cool completely.

4. Add food coloring to frosting in small bowl, a few drops at a time, until desired shade of green is reached. Frost cupcakes. Arrange marshmallows over frosting; sprinkle with sparkling sugar.

Makes 12 cupcakes

Marshmallow Delights

Little Princesses

1 package (about 18 ounces) cake mix, any flavor, plus ingredients to prepare mix
2 containers (16 ounces each) vanilla frosting
Pink, green and purple food coloring
12 mini doll picks* or 4- to 5-inch dolls
Assorted jumbo nonpareils

*Mini doll picks can be found in packages of 4 at craft stores with the cake decorating supplies.

1. Preheat oven to 350°F. Grease 24 standard (2½-inch) muffin cups. Prepare cake mix according to package directions. Spoon batter into prepared muffin cups, filling two-thirds full. Bake 18 to 20 minutes or until toothpick inserted into centers comes out clean. Cool cupcakes in pans 10 minutes; remove to wire racks to cool completely.

2. Cut off rounded tops of cupcakes with serrated knife; discard scraps. Place half of cupcakes upside down on parchment paper-lined tray or baking sheet. Spread thin layer of frosting on cupcakes. Top with remaining cupcakes, upside down. Insert doll pick into top of each cupcake stack. Trim sides of each top cupcake with serrated knife, cutting at slight angle from top to bottom, working around cupcake to create bell shape (doll's skirt). Top of cupcake should be just as wide as base of doll torso.

3. Spread thin layer of frosting over cupcakes with small offset spatula, being careful not to rip cupcake. (Frosting does not need to be completely smooth at this point, but should cover everything from doll's waist down to parchment paper.) Freeze 10 minutes to set frosting.

4. Divide remaining frosting between 3 bowls; add different food coloring to each bowl, a few drops at a time, until desired shades are reached. Frost cupcakes, completely covering first layer of frosting. Make vertical waves through frosting with mini spatula, starting in back and working around cupcake. Freeze 10 minutes to set frosting.

5. Spoon frosting into piping bags with round decorating tip or small food storage bags with small corner cut off. Pipe shirts on dolls; smooth with spatula or finger. Pipe border around dolls' waists to cover seam between shirt and skirt. Transfer to serving plates or large tray. Pipe border around bottom of cupcakes. Pipe flowers on skirts; press nonpareil into center of each flower. *Makes 12 mini cakes*

Tip: If using dolls rather than doll picks, remove the dolls' clothing and wrap the hair in plastic wrap to keep it clean while decorating.

Little Princesses

Angelic Cupcakes

   1 package (about 16 ounces) angel food cake mix
1¼ cups cold water
¼ teaspoon peppermint extract (optional)
   Red food coloring
4½ cups whipped topping

1. Preheat oven to 375°F. Line 36 standard (2½-inch) muffin cups with paper baking cups.

2. Beat cake mix, water and peppermint extract, if desired, in large bowl with electric mixer at low speed 2 minutes. Pour half of batter into medium bowl; fold in 9 drops food coloring. Alternate spoonfuls of white and pink batter in each prepared muffin cup, filling three-fourths full.

3. Bake 11 minutes or until cupcakes are golden brown with deep cracks on top. Remove to wire racks to cool completely.

4. Divide whipped topping between two small bowls. Add 2 drops food coloring to 1 bowl; stir gently until whipped topping is evenly colored. Frost cupcakes with pink and white whipped topping.

Makes 36 cupcakes

Tip Pink food coloring is available at specialty baking and craft stores; it can be used instead of red. You may need to add more than the recipe directs to reach the desired shade of pink.

Angelic Cupcakes

Friendly Frogs

1 package (about 18 ounces) cake mix, any flavor, plus ingredients to prepare mix
Green food coloring
1 container (16 ounces) vanilla frosting
Green sparkling sugar (optional)
Black round candies or candy-coated chocolate pieces
White chocolate candy discs
Black and red string licorice
Green jelly candy fruit slices (optional)

1. Preheat oven to 350°F. Line 22 standard (2½-inch) muffin cups with paper baking cups.

2. Prepare cake mix according to package directions. Spoon batter into prepared muffin cups, filling two-thirds full. Bake 18 to 22 minutes or until toothpick inserted into centers comes out clean. Cool cupcakes in pans 10 minutes; remove to wire racks to cool completely.

3. Add food coloring to frosting in small bowl, a few drops at a time, until desired shade of green is reached. Frost cupcakes; sprinkle with sparkling sugar, if desired.

4. Use small dab of frosting to attach black candies to white discs for eyes. Cut licorice into smaller lengths for mouths and noses. Arrange candies on cupcakes to create frog faces.

5. Use scissors to cut jelly candies into feet, if desired. Set cupcakes on candy feet when ready to serve.

Makes 22 cupcakes

Friendly Frogs

Under the Sea

1 package (about 18 ounces) cake mix, any flavor, plus ingredients to prepare mix
2 containers (16 ounces each) vanilla frosting
Blue, green, yellow, red and purple food coloring
White sparkling sugar (optional)
Black decorating gel
Assorted color decors, nonpareils and candy fish

1. Preheat oven to 350°F. Line 22 standard (2½-inch) muffin cups with paper baking cups or spray with nonstick cooking spray.

2. Prepare cake mix according to package directions. Spoon batter into prepared muffin cups, filling two-thirds full. Bake 18 to 22 minutes or until toothpick inserted into centers comes out clean. Cool cupcakes in pans 10 minutes; remove to wire racks to cool completely.

3. Place 1 container frosting in small bowl; add blue and green food coloring, a few drops at a time, until desired shade of aqua is reached. Spoon into pastry bag with large star decorating tip. Pipe aqua frosting in swirl pattern on cupcakes. Sprinkle with sparkling sugar, if desired.

4. Divide remaining frosting between 4 bowls; add different food coloring (except blue) to each bowl, a few drops at a time, until desired shades are reached. Spoon each color into pastry bags with round decorating tip or small food storage bags with small corner cut off. Pipe sea creatures and plants on cupcakes: yellow fish, red lobsters, purple starfish and green seaweed. Decorate with decorating gel, decors and candies.

Makes 22 cupcakes

Under the Sea

Pretty in Pink

2 cups all-purpose flour
1 teaspoon baking soda
1 teaspoon baking powder
½ teaspoon salt
½ cup sour cream
½ cup milk
1 teaspoon vanilla
1 cup granulated sugar
½ cup (1 stick) butter, softened
2 eggs
2 to 3 tablespoons multi-colored cake decors (sprinkles)
Pink food coloring
1 container (16 ounces) vanilla frosting
12 small tiaras
White and pink sparkling sugars

1. Preheat oven to 350°F. Line 12 standard (2½-inch) muffin cups with paper baking cups. Sift flour, baking soda, baking powder and salt into medium bowl. Combine sour cream, milk and vanilla in small bowl until well blended.

2. Beat granulated sugar and butter in large bowl with electric mixer at medium speed 2 minutes or until fluffy. Add eggs, 1 at a time, beating well after each addition. Add flour mixture alternately with sour cream mixture, beginning and ending with flour mixture, beating well after each addition. Stir in decors until blended. Spoon batter evenly into prepared muffin cups.

3. Bake 21 to 23 minutes or until toothpick inserted into centers comes out clean. Cool cupcakes in pan 5 minutes; remove to wire rack to cool completely

4. Stir food coloring into frosting in small bowl, a few drops at a time, until desired shade of pink is reached. Pipe or spread frosting on cupcakes. Arrange tiaras on cupcakes; sprinkle with sparkling sugars.

Makes 12 cupcakes

Pretty in Pink

Dragonflies

1 package (about 18 ounces) cake mix, any flavor, plus ingredients to prepare mix
White confectionery coating*
Pink, purple, yellow and green food coloring
44 small pretzel twists
22 pretzel sticks (about 3 inches)
1 container (16 ounces) vanilla frosting
White and purple nonpareils
Silver dragees

Confectionery coating, also called almond bark or candy coating, can be found at craft stores and in the baking section of the supermarket. It comes in blocks, discs and chips and is usually available in white, milk and dark chocolate varieties.

1. Preheat oven to 350°F. Line 22 standard (2½-inch) muffin cups with paper baking cups.

2. Prepare cake mix according to package directions. Spoon batter into prepared muffin cups, filling two-thirds full. Bake 18 to 22 minutes or until toothpick inserted into centers comes out clean. Cool cupcakes in pans 10 minutes; remove to wire racks to cool completely.

3. Line large baking sheet with waxed paper. Melt confectionary coating according to package directions. Stir in pink food coloring, a few drops at a time, until desired shade of pink is reached. Dip pretzel twists in melted candy to coat; arrange 2 twists together on prepared baking sheet. Dip pretzel sticks in melted candy; place 1 stick between 2 pretzel twists to create dragonfly. Sprinkle pretzel twists with white nonpareils; arrange 2 purple nonpareils at top of pretzel sticks for eyes. Press dragees into bottom half of pretzel sticks. Let stand 10 minutes or until set.

4. Meanwhile, divide frosting between 3 small bowls. Add different food coloring (except pink) to each bowl, a few drops at a time, until desired shades are reached. Pipe or spread frosting on cupcakes; top with dragonflies.   *Makes 22 cupcakes*

Dragonflies

Just Plain Fun

Sunny Side Upcakes

1 package (about 18 ounces) vanilla cake mix, plus ingredients to prepare mix
22 yellow chewy fruit candies
2 containers (16 ounces each) vanilla frosting

1. Preheat oven to 350°F. Line 22 standard (2½-inch) muffin cups with paper baking cups.

2. Prepare cake mix according to package directions. Spoon batter into prepared muffin cups, filling two-thirds full. Bake 18 to 22 minutes or until toothpick inserted into centers comes out clean. Cool cupcakes in pans 10 minutes; remove to wire racks to cool completely.

3. For each egg yolk, microwave candy on LOW (30%) 5 seconds or just until softened. Shape into ball; flatten slightly.

4. Place 1 cup frosting in small microwavable bowl; microwave on LOW (30%) 10 seconds or until softened. Working with 1 cupcake at a time, spoon about 2 tablespoons frosting in center of cupcake. Spread frosting toward edges of cupcake in uneven petal shapes to resemble egg white. Press candy into frosting in center of cupcake. Microwave additional frosting as needed.

Makes 22 cupcakes

Cookie in a Cupcake

1 package (16 ounces) refrigerated break-apart chocolate chip cookie dough (24 count), divided
2 cups all-purpose flour
½ cup unsweetened cocoa powder
1 teaspoon baking soda
½ teaspoon salt
½ cup (1 stick) butter, softened
1 cup sugar
1 egg
1 teaspoon vanilla
½ cup sour cream
½ cup hot water

1. Preheat oven to 350°F. Place 12 standard (2-inch) silicone muffin cups on large baking sheet or line 12 standard (2½-inch) muffin cups with paper baking cups.

2. Break apart half of cookie dough into 12 pieces along score lines. (Reserve remaining half of dough for another use.) Roll each piece of dough into a ball; refrigerate balls of dough while preparing cupcake batter.

3. Sift flour, cocoa, baking soda and salt into medium bowl. Beat butter in large bowl with electric mixer about 2 minutes or until creamy. Add sugar; beat 2 to 3 minutes or until light and fluffy. Beat in egg until well blended. Beat in vanilla.

4. Add sour cream and water to butter mixture alternately with flour mixture, beginning and ending with flour mixture. Beat until blended. Spoon batter evenly into prepared muffin cups. Place 1 ball of cookie dough into each cup, pressing down into batter.

5. Bake 20 to 22 minutes or until toothpick inserted into cake portion of cupcake comes out clean. Cool cupcakes in pan 5 minutes; remove to wire rack to cool slightly. Serve warm.

Makes 12 cupcakes

Cookie in a Cupcake

Hot Chocolate Cupcakes

1 package (about 16 ounces) pound cake mix, plus ingredients to prepare mix
4 containers (4 ounces each) prepared chocolate pudding*
2½ cups whipped topping, divided
4 small chewy chocolate candies
Unsweetened cocoa powder (optional)

*Or, purchase 1 (4-serving size) package instant chocolate pudding and pie filling mix and prepare according to package directions. Use 2 cups pudding for recipe; reserve remaining pudding for another use.

1. Preheat oven to 350°F. Spray 15 standard (2½-inch) muffin cups with baking spray (nonstick cooking spray with flour added) or grease and flour cups. Prepare cake mix according to package directions. Spoon batter into prepared muffin cups, filling about two-thirds full.

2. Bake 20 to 25 minutes or until toothpick inserted into centers comes out clean. Cool cupcakes in pans 5 minutes; remove to wire racks to cool completely.

3. Combine chocolate pudding and 2 cups whipped topping in medium bowl until well blended; refrigerate until ready to use.

4. Microwave chocolate candies on LOW (30%) 5 to 10 seconds or until slightly softened. Stretch each candy into long thin rope; cut ropes into 2-inch lengths. Curve candy pieces into "C" shape to resemble handles of mugs, pressing both ends of each handle to flatten slightly.

5. Cut out 2-inch circle about 1 inch deep from top of each cupcake with small paring knife. Cut 2 slits ½ inch apart in one side of each cupcake with small paring knife. Insert chocolate candy into slits to resemble mug handle. Fill hole in each cupcake with chocolate pudding mixture. Top with small dollop of remaining whipped topping; sprinkle with cocoa, if desired.

Makes 15 cupcakes

Hot Chocolate Cupcakes

Marshmallow Fudge Sundae Cupcakes

  1 package (about 18 ounces) chocolate cake mix, plus ingredients to prepare mix
  2 packages (4 ounces each) waffle bowls
40 large marshmallows
  1 jar (8 ounces) hot fudge topping
    Colored sprinkles or chopped nuts
1¼ cups whipped topping
  1 jar (10 ounces) maraschino cherries

1. Preheat oven to 350°F. Lightly spray 20 standard (2½-inch) muffin cups with nonstick cooking spray.

2. Prepare cake mix according to package directions. Spoon batter into prepared muffin cups, filling three-fourths full. Bake 20 to 22 minutes or until toothpick inserted into centers comes out clean. Cool cupcakes in pans 10 minutes; remove to wire racks to cool completely.

3. Place waffle bowls on ungreased baking sheets. Place one cupcake in each waffle bowl. Top each cupcake with 2 marshmallows; return to oven 2 minutes or until marshmallows are slightly softened.

4. Remove lid from hot fudge topping; microwave on HIGH 10 seconds or until softened. Top each cupcake with hot fudge topping, sprinkles, whipped topping and cherry.

Makes 20 cupcakes

Marshmallow Fudge Sundae Cupcakes

Margarita Cupcakes

        1 package (about 18 ounces) white cake mix
    ¾ cup plus 2 tablespoons margarita mix, divided
        2 eggs
    ⅓ cup vegetable oil
    ¼ cup water
        1 tablespoon grated lime peel (about 3 limes), divided
        Juice of 1 lime
        2 tablespoons tequila or lime juice
        3 cups powdered sugar
        1 tablespoon sparkling or granulated sugar
        1 tablespoon salt (optional)
        Green and yellow food coloring
        Lime peel strips (optional)

1. Preheat oven to 350°F. Line 22 standard (2½-inch) muffin cups with paper baking cups.

2. Combine cake mix, ¾ cup margarita mix, eggs, oil, water, 1 teaspoon lime peel and lime juice in large bowl. Whisk 2 minutes or until well blended. Spoon batter into prepared muffin cups, filling two-thirds full.

3. Bake 20 to 25 minutes or until toothpick inserted into centers comes out clean. Cool cupcakes in pans 5 minutes; remove to wire racks to cool completely.

4. Combine tequila, remaining 2 tablespoons margarita mix and 2 teaspoons lime peel in medium bowl. Gradually whisk in powdered sugar until desired glaze consistency is reached. Combine sparkling sugar and salt, if desired, in small bowl. Add food coloring, a few drops at a time, until desired shade of green is reached.

5. Spread glaze over cupcakes; dip edges in sugar-salt mixture. Garnish with lime peel strips.

Makes 22 cupcakes

Margarita Cupcakes

Quick Cookie Cupcakes

1 package (16 ounces) refrigerated break-apart chocolate chip cookie dough (24 count)
1½ cups chocolate frosting
Colored decors

1. Preheat oven to 350°F. Line 24 mini (1¾-inch) muffin cups with paper baking cups.

2. Break dough into 24 pieces along score lines. Roll each piece into a ball; place in prepared muffin cups. Bake 10 to 12 minutes or until golden brown. Cool cupcakes in pans 5 minutes; remove to wire racks to cool completely.

3. Pipe or spread frosting over each cupcake; sprinkle with decors.

Makes 24 mini cupcakes

Tip These cupcakes are perfect for every occasion—they can be made in just minutes, and you can change the paper baking cups and decorations to match your theme. Use pink colors for Valentine's Day; green for St. Patrick's Day; red, white and blue for the 4th of July; and school colors for graduation parties. Craft stores usually stock baking cups and cake decorations in seasonal colors and patterns.

Quick Cookie Cupcakes

Cupcake Sliders

　　2 cups all-purpose flour
2½ teaspoons baking powder
　½ teaspoon salt
　1 cup milk
　½ teaspoon vanilla
1½ cups sugar
　½ cup (1 stick) butter, softened
　3 eggs
1¼ cups chocolate hazelnut spread or milk chocolate frosting

1. Preheat oven to 350°F. Spray 18 standard (2½-inch) muffin cups with nonstick cooking spray.

2. Combine flour, baking powder and salt in medium bowl. Combine milk and vanilla in measuring cup. Beat sugar and butter in large bowl with electric mixer at medium speed about 3 minutes or until creamy. Add eggs, 1 at a time, beating well after each addition. Add flour mixture alternately with milk mixture, ending with flour mixture, beating until well blended. Spoon batter into prepared muffin cups, filling three-fourths full.

3. Bake 18 to 20 minutes or until toothpick inserted into centers comes out clean. Cool cupcakes in pans 10 minutes; remove to wire racks to cool completely.

4. Cut off edges of cupcakes to form squares. Cut cupcakes in half crosswise. Spread each bottom half with about 1 tablespoon chocolate hazelnut spread; replace tops of cupcakes.

Makes 18 cupcakes

Cupcake Sliders

Iced Coffee Cupcakes

   1 package (about 18 ounces) chocolate fudge cake mix *without* pudding in the mix
   1 package (4-serving size) instant chocolate pudding and pie filling mix
1⅓ cups brewed coffee, cooled to room temperature
   3 eggs
½ cup vegetable oil
   1 teaspoon vanilla
½ gallon mocha almond fudge or coffee ice cream, softened
   1 bottle (7¼ ounces) quick-hardening chocolate shell dessert topping
½ cup pecan pieces, toasted*

To toast pecans, spread in single layer on baking sheet. Bake in preheated 350°F oven 5 to 7 minutes or until fragrant, stirring frequently.

1. Preheat oven to 350°F. Line 22 standard (2½-inch) muffin cups with foil or paper baking cups or spray with nonstick cooking spray.

2. Beat cake mix, pudding mix, coffee, eggs, oil and vanilla in large bowl with electric mixer at low speed 30 seconds. Beat at medium speed 2 minutes or until well blended and fluffy. Spoon batter into prepared muffin cups, filling two-thirds full.

3. Bake 18 to 22 minutes or until toothpick inserted into centers comes out clean. Cool cupcakes in pans 10 minutes; remove to wire racks to cool completely.

4. Remove 1 tablespoon cake from center of 1 cupcake. Fill hole with 2 to 3 tablespoons ice cream, mounding slightly. Spoon about 1 tablespoon chocolate shell topping over ice cream; quickly sprinkle with pecans before topping hardens. Place cupcake in freezer until ready to serve. Repeat with remaining cupcakes, ice cream, topping and pecans.

Makes 22 cupcakes

Iced Coffee Cupcakes

Crispy Cupcakes

¼ cup (½ stick) plus 2 tablespoons butter, divided
1 package (10½ ounces) marshmallows
½ cup creamy peanut butter
6 cups crisp rice cereal
1 cup bittersweet or semisweet chocolate chips
1½ cups powdered sugar
¼ cup milk

1. Spray 13×9-inch baking pan with nonstick cooking spray. Microwave 2 tablespoons butter in large microwavable bowl on HIGH 30 seconds or until melted. Add marshmallows; stir until coated with butter. Microwave on HIGH 1 minute; stir. Microwave 45 seconds; stir until melted. Stir in peanut butter until well blended. Add cereal; stir until blended.

2. Spread mixture in prepared pan, using waxed paper to spread and press into even layer. Let stand 10 to 15 minutes until set.

3. Meanwhile, place remaining ¼ cup butter and chocolate chips in medium microwavable bowl. Microwave on HIGH 40 seconds; stir. Microwave at additional 15-second intervals until melted and smooth. Gradually beat in powdered sugar and milk until well blended. Refrigerate frosting until ready to use.

4. Spray 1½-inch round cookie or biscuit cutter with nonstick cooking spray; cut out 36 circles from cereal bars. Place small dab of frosting on top of 18 circles; top with remaining 18 circles, pressing down firmly to seal. Place "cupcakes" in paper baking cups, if desired. Pipe or spread frosting on cupcakes.

Makes 18 cupcakes

Crispy Cupcakes

Peanut Butter & Jelly Cupcakes

  1 package (about 18 ounces) yellow cake mix, plus ingredients to prepare mix
¾ cup creamy peanut butter
½ cup (1 stick) butter, softened
  2 cups powdered sugar
½ teaspoon vanilla
¼ cup milk
  2 cups strawberry jelly

1. Preheat oven to 350°F. Line 22 standard (2½-inch) muffin cups with paper baking cups.

2. Prepare cake mix according to package directions. Spoon batter into prepared muffin cups, filling two-thirds full. Bake 18 to 22 minutes or until toothpick inserted into centers comes out clean. Cool cupcakes in pans 10 minutes; remove to wire racks to cool completely.

3. Beat peanut butter and butter in medium bowl with electric mixer at medium speed 2 minutes or until smooth. Add sugar and vanilla; beat at low speed 1 minute or until crumbly. Slowly add milk, beating at low speed until creamy.

4. Fill pastry bag fitted with small decorator tip with jelly. Insert tip into top of cupcake; squeeze bag gently to fill center of cupcake with jelly. (Stop squeezing when you feel resistance or jelly comes out of top of cupcake.) Repeat with remaining cupcakes and jelly.

5. Pipe or spread peanut butter frosting decoratively on cupcakes.   *Makes 22 cupcakes*

Peanut Butter & Jelly Cupcakes

Red Velvet Cupcakes

2¼ cups all-purpose flour
1 teaspoon salt
2 bottles (1 ounce each) red food coloring
3 tablespoons unsweetened cocoa powder
1 cup buttermilk
1 teaspoon vanilla
1½ cups sugar
½ cup (1 stick) butter, softened
2 eggs
1 teaspoon white vinegar
1 teaspoon baking soda
1 to 2 containers (16 ounces each) whipped cream cheese frosting
Toasted coconut* (optional)

To toast coconut, spread evenly on ungreased baking sheet. Bake in preheated 350°F oven 5 to 7 minutes or until light golden brown, stirring occasionally.

1. Preheat oven to 350°F. Line 18 standard (2½-inch) muffin cups with paper baking cups.

2. Combine flour and salt in medium bowl. Gradually stir food coloring into cocoa in small bowl until blended and smooth. Combine buttermilk and vanilla in separate bowl.

3. Beat sugar and butter in large bowl with electric mixer at medium speed about 4 minutes or until very light and fluffy. Add eggs, 1 at a time, beating well after each addition. Add cocoa mixture; beat until well blended and uniform in color. Add flour mixture alternately with buttermilk mixture, beating just until blended. Combine vinegar and baking soda in small bowl; gently fold into batter with spatula or spoon (do not use mixer). Spoon batter into prepared muffin cups, filling two-thirds full.

4. Bake 18 to 20 minutes or until toothpick inserted into centers comes out clean. Cool cupcakes in pans 10 minutes; remove to wire racks to cool completely.

5. Generously spread frosting over cupcakes. Sprinkle with coconut, if desired.

Makes 18 cupcakes

Red Velvet Cupcakes

Black & Whites

1 package (about 18 ounces) vanilla cake mix, plus ingredients to prepare mix
⅔ cup semisweet chocolate chips, melted
4 ounces cream cheese, softened
1 cup prepared vanilla frosting
1 cup prepared chocolate frosting

1. Preheat oven to 350°F. Line 22 standard (2½-inch) muffin cups with paper baking cups.

2. Prepare cake mix according to package directions. Reserve 2½ cups batter in medium bowl. Add melted chocolate and cream cheese to remaining batter; beat with electric mixer at medium speed about 2 minutes or until smooth and well blended.

3. Spoon chocolate and vanilla batters side by side into prepared muffin cups, filling about two-thirds full. (Use chocolate batter first as it is slightly thicker and easier to position on one side of muffin cups.)

4. Bake 16 to 18 minutes or until toothpick inserted into centers comes out clean. Cool cupcakes in pans 10 minutes; remove to wire racks to cool completely.

5. Spread vanilla frosting over half of each cupcake; spread chocolate frosting over remaining half of each cupcake.

Makes 22 cupcakes

Black & Whites

Mini Doughnut Cupcakes

1 cup sugar
1½ teaspoons ground cinnamon
1 package (about 18 ounces) yellow or white cake mix, plus ingredients to prepare mix
1 tablespoon ground nutmeg

1. Preheat oven to 350°F. Grease and flour 48 mini (1¾-inch) muffin cups. Combine sugar and cinnamon in small bowl; set aside.

2. Prepare cake mix according to package directions; stir in nutmeg. Spoon batter into prepared muffin cups, filling two-thirds full.

3. Bake about 12 minutes or until lightly browned and toothpick inserted into centers comes out clean.

4. Remove cupcakes from pans. Roll warm cupcakes in sugar mixture until completely coated.   *Makes 48 mini cupcakes*

Note: These cupcakes are best served the day they are made.

Tip Save any remaining cinnamon-sugar mixture to sprinkle on toast and pancakes.

Mini Doughnut Cupcakes

Peanut Butter & Milk Chocolate Cupcakes

1 package (about 18 ounces) butter recipe yellow cake mix with pudding in the mix, plus ingredients to prepare mix

$\frac{1}{2}$ cup creamy peanut butter

$\frac{1}{4}$ cup ($\frac{1}{2}$ stick) butter, softened

2 bars ($3\frac{1}{2}$ ounces each) high-quality milk chocolate, broken into small pieces

$\frac{1}{4}$ cup ($\frac{1}{2}$ stick) butter, cut into small chunks

$\frac{1}{4}$ cup whipping cream

Dash salt

Peanut butter chips

1. Preheat oven to 350°F. Line 22 standard (2½-inch) muffin cups with paper baking cups.

2. Prepare cake mix according to package directions, using ½ cup peanut butter and ¼ cup softened butter instead of ½ cup butter called for in package directions. Spoon batter evenly into prepared muffin cups, filling two-thirds full.

3. Bake 24 to 26 minutes or until light golden brown and toothpick inserted into centers comes out clean. Cool cupcakes in pans 10 minutes; remove to wire racks to cool completely.

4. Combine chocolate, remaining ¼ cup butter, cream and salt in small, heavy saucepan. Heat over low heat, stirring constantly, just until butter and chocolate are melted. (Mixture should be warm, not hot.) Immediately spoon about 1 tablespoon chocolate glaze over each cupcake, spreading to cover top. Sprinkle with peanut butter chips. *Makes 22 cupcakes*

Peanut Butter & Milk Chocolate Cupcakes

Fruit Follies

Pink Lemonade Cupcakes

  1 package (about 18 ounces) white cake mix *without* pudding in the mix
  1 cup water
  3 egg whites
 ⅓ cup plus ¼ cup thawed frozen pink lemonade concentrate, divided
  2 tablespoons vegetable oil
  5 to 8 drops red food coloring, divided
  4 cups powdered sugar
 ⅓ cup (⅔ stick) butter, softened
    Lemon slice candies (optional)

1. Preheat oven to 350°F. Line 22 standard (2½-inch) muffin cups with paper baking cups.

2. Beat cake mix, water, egg whites, ⅓ cup lemonade concentrate, oil and 4 to 6 drops food coloring in large bowl with electric mixer at medium speed 2 minutes or until well blended. Spoon batter into prepared muffin cups, filling two-thirds full.

3. Bake 18 to 22 minutes or until toothpick inserted into centers comes out clean. Cool cupcakes in pans 5 minutes; remove to wire racks to cool completely.

4. Beat powdered sugar, butter and remaining ¼ cup lemonade concentrate in medium bowl with electric mixer at medium speed until well blended. Beat in remaining 1 to 2 drops food coloring until desired shade of pink is reached.

5. Spread frosting over cupcakes; garnish with candies and straws.   *Makes 22 cupcakes*

Banana Cupcakes

2 cups all-purpose flour
1½ cups granulated sugar
2 tablespoons packed brown sugar
2 teaspoons baking powder
½ teaspoon salt
½ teaspoon ground cinnamon
¼ teaspoon ground allspice
½ cup vegetable oil
2 eggs
¼ cup milk
1 teaspoon vanilla
2 mashed bananas (about 1 cup)
1 container (16 ounces) chocolate frosting
Chocolate sprinkles (optional)

1. Preheat oven to 350°F. Line 18 standard (2½-inch) muffin cups with paper baking cups.

2. Combine flour, granulated sugar, brown sugar, baking powder, salt, cinnamon and allspice in large bowl. Add oil, eggs, milk and vanilla; beat with electric mixer at medium speed 2 minutes or until well blended. Beat in bananas until well blended. Spoon batter into prepared muffin cups, filling three-fourths full.

3. Bake 25 to 30 minutes or until toothpick inserted into centers comes out clean. Cool cupcakes in pans 10 minutes; remove to wire racks to cool completely.

4. Frost cupcakes; decorate with sprinkles, if desired.   *Makes 18 cupcakes*

Banana Cupcakes

Key Lime Pie Cupcakes

 1 package (about 18 ounces) lemon cake mix with pudding in the mix
 1 cup vegetable oil
 4 eggs
 ¾ cup key lime juice,* divided
 ½ cup water
 1 teaspoon grated lime peel
 2 cups whipping cream
 ½ cup powdered sugar
  Lime wedges or additional grated lime peel (optional)

If key lime juice is not available, substitute regular lime juice.

1. Preheat oven to 350°F. Line 22 standard (2½-inch) muffin cups with paper baking cups.

2. Combine cake mix, oil, eggs, ½ cup key lime juice, water and lime peel in large bowl; whisk 2 minutes or until thick and smooth. Spoon batter into prepared muffin cups, filling two-thirds full.

3. Bake 19 to 23 minutes or until toothpick inserted into centers comes out clean. Cool cupcakes in pans 10 minutes; remove to wire racks to cool completely.

4. Beat cream in medium bowl with electric mixer at medium speed 3 to 5 minutes or until soft peaks form. Add sugar and remaining ¼ cup key lime juice; beat at medium-high speed 30 seconds or until medium-stiff peaks form.

5. Top each cupcake with dollop of whipped cream. Garnish with lime wedges. Serve immediately. *Makes 22 cupcakes*

Key Lime Pie Cupcakes

Strawberry Short Cupcakes

    2 cups all-purpose flour
2½ teaspoons baking powder
 ½ teaspoon salt
   1 cup milk
   1 teaspoon vanilla
1½ cups plus 3 tablespoons sugar, divided
 ½ cup (1 stick) butter, softened
   3 eggs
1½ cups cold whipping cream
   2 quarts fresh strawberries, sliced

1. Preheat oven to 350°F. Spray 18 standard (2½-inch) muffin cups with nonstick cooking spray.

2. Combine flour, baking powder and salt in medium bowl. Combine milk and vanilla in small bowl. Beat 1½ cups sugar and butter in large bowl with electric mixer at medium speed about 3 minutes or until creamy. Add eggs, 1 at a time, beating well after each addition. Add flour mixture alternately with milk mixture, beating until well blended. Spoon batter into prepared muffin cups, filling about three-fourths full.

3. Bake 18 to 20 minutes or until toothpick inserted into centers comes out clean. Cool cupcakes in pans 10 minutes; remove to wire racks to cool completely.

4. Beat cream in large bowl with electric mixer at high speed until soft peaks form. Gradually add remaining 3 tablespoons sugar; beat until stiff peaks form.

5. Cut cupcakes in half crosswise. Top each bottom half with about 2 tablespoons whipped cream and strawberries. Replace top half; top with additional whipped cream and strawberries.

Makes 18 cupcakes

Strawberry Short Cupcake

Lemon Meringue Cupcakes

1 package (about 18 ounces) lemon cake mix, plus ingredients to prepare mix
¾ cup prepared lemon curd*
4 egg whites, at room temperature
6 tablespoons sugar

Lemon curd, a thick sweet lemon spread, is available in many supermarkets near the jams and preserves.

1. Preheat oven to 350°F. Line 9 jumbo (3½-inch) muffin cups with paper baking cups.

2. Prepare cake mix according to package directions. Spoon batter into prepared muffin cups, filling two-thirds full. Bake 23 to 25 minutes or until toothpick inserted into centers comes out clean. Cool cupcakes in pans 10 minutes; remove to wire racks to cool completely. *Increase oven temperature to 375°F.*

3. Cut off tops of cupcakes with serrated knife. (Do not remove paper baking cups.) Scoop out small hole in center of each cupcake with tablespoon; fill hole with generous tablespoon lemon curd. Replace cupcake tops.

4. Beat egg whites in medium bowl with electric mixer at high speed until soft peaks form. Continue beating while gradually adding sugar; beat until stiff peaks form. Pipe or spread meringue in peaks on each cupcake.

5. Place cupcakes on baking sheet. Bake 5 to 6 minutes or until peaks of meringue are golden.

Makes 9 jumbo cupcakes

Variation: This recipe also makes 22 standard (2½-inch) cupcakes. Line muffin pans with paper baking cups; prepare and bake cake mix according to package directions. Cut off tops of cupcakes; scoop out hole in each cupcake with teaspoon and fill with generous teaspoon lemon curd. Pipe or spread about ⅓ cup meringue in peaks on each cupcake; bake as directed.

Lemon Meringue Cupcakes

Blueberry Cheesecake Cupcakes

  1 package (16 ounces) refrigerated mini break-apart sugar cookie dough (40 count)*
  2 packages (8 ounces each) cream cheese, softened
  1 cup sugar
  2 eggs
  1 tablespoon cornstarch
  1½ teaspoons vanilla
  3 egg whites
  ½ teaspoon cream of tartar
  ¼ cup blueberry preserves
  1 pint fresh blueberries (optional)

If mini size cookie dough is not available, substitute regular size cookie dough (20 count) and use 1 piece of dough per cupcake instead of 2 pieces.

1. Preheat oven to 325°F. Line 20 standard (2½-inch) muffin cups with foil baking cups; lightly spray with nonstick cooking spray. Break off 2 cookie pieces from refrigerated dough. Roll into a ball, flatten slightly and press into bottom of baking cup. Repeat with remaining cookie dough. Bake 10 minutes. Immediately press down center of each cookie with back of spoon to flatten.

2. Beat cream cheese in large bowl with electric mixer at medium speed until smooth. Add sugar, eggs, cornstarch and vanilla; beat until smooth and well blended.

3. Beat egg whites and cream of tartar in medium bowl with electric mixer at high speed until stiff peaks form. Stir half of egg white mixture into cream cheese mixture. Gently fold in remaining egg white mixture until just combined. Swirl in blueberry preserves. *Do not overmix.* Spoon batter evenly over cooled cookie crusts.

4. Bake 17 to 20 minutes. (Centers will be spongy.) Cool cupcakes in pans 10 minutes; place pans in refrigerator to cool completely. Store in airtight container until ready to serve. Garnish with blueberries. *Makes 20 cupcakes*

Note: It is important to use foil baking cups rather than paper ones because they provide extra structure for the cheesecake.

Blueberry Cheesecake Cupcake

Raspberry Streusel Cupcakes

    Streusel Topping (recipe follows)
 3 cups all-purpose flour
 2 teaspoons baking powder
½ teaspoon salt
⅛ teaspoon ground cinnamon
1½ cups sugar
½ cup (1 stick) butter, softened
 2 eggs
 1 teaspoon vanilla
 1 cup sour cream
1½ pints fresh raspberries

1. Preheat oven to 350°F. Line 24 standard (2½-inch) muffin cups with paper baking cups. Prepare Streusel Topping; set aside.

2. Whisk flour, baking powder, salt and cinnamon in medium bowl. Beat sugar and butter in large bowl with electric mixer at medium speed 2 to 3 minutes or until light and fluffy. Add eggs, 1 at a time, beating well after each addition. Stir in vanilla. Add flour mixture alternately with sour cream, beating just until blended. Gently fold in raspberries. Spoon evenly into prepared muffin cups; sprinkle with Streusel Topping.

3. Bake 20 to 25 minutes or until toothpick inserted into centers comes out clean. Cool cupcakes in pans 10 minutes; remove to wire racks to cool completely.

Makes 24 cupcakes

Streusel Topping: Combine 1 cup sugar, ⅔ cup all-purpose flour, ¼ cup pecan chips, 1 teaspoon ground cinnamon and ¼ teaspoon salt in medium bowl. Cut ½ cup (1 stick) butter into small pieces; cut butter and 1 tablespoon milk into sugar mixture with pastry blender or 2 knives until mixture resembles coarse crumbs.

Raspberry Streusel Cupcakes

Cha-Cha-Cha Chocolate

Mini Turtle Cupcakes

  1 package (21½ ounces) brownie mix, plus ingredients to prepare mix
½ cup chopped pecans
  1 container (16 ounces) dark chocolate frosting
½ cup coarsely chopped pecans, toasted
12 caramels
  1 to 2 tablespoons whipping cream

1. Heat oven to 350°F. Line 54 mini (1½-inch) muffin cups with paper baking cups.

2. Prepare brownie mix according to package directions; stir in chopped pecans. Spoon batter into prepared muffin cups, filling two-thirds full.

3. Bake 18 minutes or until toothpick inserted into centers comes out clean. Cool cupcakes in pans 10 minutes; remove to wire racks to cool completely. (At this point, cupcakes may be frozen up to 3 months. Thaw at room temperature before frosting.)

4. Frost cupcakes; top with toasted pecans.

5. Heat caramels and 1 tablespoon cream in small saucepan over low heat until caramels are melted and mixture is smooth, stirring frequently. Add additional 1 tablespoon cream, if necessary, to thin mixture. Spoon caramel evenly over cupcakes. Store at room temperature up to 24 hours or cover and refrigerate up to 3 days. *Makes 54 mini cupcakes*

Black Bottom Cupcakes

- 1 package (8 ounces) cream cheese, softened
- 4 eggs, divided
- $\frac{1}{3}$ cup plus $\frac{1}{2}$ cup granulated sugar, divided
- 2 cups all-purpose flour
- 1 cup packed brown sugar
- $\frac{3}{4}$ cup unsweetened cocoa powder
- 1 teaspoon baking powder
- $\frac{1}{2}$ teaspoon baking soda
- $\frac{1}{2}$ teaspoon salt
- 1 cup buttermilk
- $\frac{1}{2}$ cup vegetable oil
- $1\frac{1}{2}$ teaspoons vanilla

1. Preheat oven to 350°F. Line 20 standard (2½-inch) muffin cups with paper or foil baking cups. Beat cream cheese, 1 egg and ⅓ cup granulated sugar in small bowl with electric mixer at medium speed until smooth and creamy; set aside.

2. Combine flour, brown sugar, cocoa, remaining ½ cup granulated sugar, baking powder, baking soda and salt in large bowl; mix well. Beat buttermilk, remaining 3 eggs, oil and vanilla in medium bowl until well blended. Add buttermilk mixture to flour mixture; beat about 2 minutes or until well blended.

3. Spoon batter into prepared muffin cups, filling about three-fourths full. Spoon heaping tablespoon cream cheese mixture over batter in each cup; gently swirl with tip of knife to marbleize.

4. Bake 20 to 25 minutes or until toothpick inserted into centers comes out clean. Cool cupcakes in pans 5 minutes; remove to wire racks to cool completely.   *Makes 20 cupcakes*

Black Bottom Cupcakes

S'More-Topped Cupcakes

- 1¼ cups all-purpose flour
- ½ cup unsweetened cocoa powder
- ¾ teaspoon baking soda
- ½ teaspoon salt
- ½ cup (1 stick) butter, softened
- 1¼ cups sugar
- 2 eggs
- 1 cup milk
- 1 teaspoon vanilla
- 6 whole graham crackers (12 squares)
- 1½ cups marshmallow creme
- 1½ bars (3 to 4 ounces each) milk chocolate, chopped into ½-inch chunks

1. Preheat oven to 350°F. Line 12 standard (2½-inch) muffin cups with paper baking cups. Sift flour, cocoa, baking soda and salt into medium bowl.

2. Beat butter in large bowl with electric mixer at medium speed until creamy and light. Add sugar; beat 3 minutes. Add eggs, 1 at a time, beating well after each addition. Combine milk and vanilla. Add flour mixture and milk mixture alternately to batter, beginning and ending with flour mixture. Spoon batter into prepared muffin cups, filling three-fourths full.

3. Bake 21 to 24 minutes or until toothpick inserted into centers comes out clean. Cool cupcakes in pan 5 minutes; remove to wire rack to cool completely.

4. Break each graham cracker square into ¾-inch pieces; press onto each cupcake to completely cover top and extend slightly over edge of cupcake. Spread about 2 tablespoons marshmallow creme over each cupcake (see Tip); top with chocolate chunks. Freeze cupcakes 15 minutes.

5. Preheat broiler. Place cupcakes on baking sheet. Broil cupcakes at least 6 inches from heat source about 1 minute or until marshmallow creme is lightly browned. Serve immediately.

Makes 12 cupcakes

Tip: Marshmallow creme is very sticky and can be difficult to spread. Spray your utensils with nonstick cooking spray; drop teaspoon-size dollops of marshmallow creme over graham crackers and spread gently to cover.

S'More-Topped Cupcakes

Fudgy Mocha Cupcakes with Chocolate Coffee Ganache

1 package (about 18 ounces) devil's food cake mix *without* pudding in the mix
1 package (4-serving size) chocolate fudge instant pudding and pie filling mix
1⅓ cups strong brewed coffee, at room temperature
3 eggs
½ cup vegetable oil
6 ounces semisweet chocolate, finely chopped
½ cup whipping cream
2 teaspoons instant coffee granules
½ cup prepared vanilla frosting

1. Preheat oven to 350°F. Line 22 standard (2½-inch) muffin cups with paper baking cups.

2. Beat cake mix, pudding mix, coffee, eggs and oil in large bowl with electric mixer at medium speed 2 minutes or until well blended. Spoon batter into prepared muffin cups, filling two-thirds full.

3. Bake 22 to 24 minutes or until toothpick inserted into centers comes out clean. Cool cupcakes in pans 10 minutes; remove to wire racks to cool completely.

4. For ganache, place chocolate in small bowl. Heat cream and instant coffee in small saucepan over medium-low heat until bubbles appear around edge of pan. Pour cream over chocolate; let stand about 2 minutes. Stir until mixture is smooth and shiny. Let ganache cool completely. (Ganache will be slightly runny.)

5. Dip tops of cupcakes into ganache; smooth surface. Place frosting in pastry bag fitted with small round writing tip. Pipe letters on cupcakes.   *Makes 22 cupcakes*

Fudgy Mocha Cupcakes with Chocolate Coffee Ganache

Tiramisu Cupcakes

        2 teaspoons instant coffee or espresso powder
        1 tablespoon hot water
        1 tablespoon coffee liqueur
        1 package (about 18 ounces) yellow butter recipe cake mix
        3 eggs
    $\frac{2}{3}$ cup water
    $\frac{1}{2}$ cup (1 stick) butter, softened and cut into small pieces
        1 package (8 ounces) mascarpone cheese*
    $\frac{1}{2}$ cup powdered sugar
    $\frac{1}{4}$ teaspoon vanilla
    $\frac{1}{2}$ container (8 ounces) French vanilla whipped topping
        Unsweetened cocoa powder

Mascarpone cheese is an Italian soft cheese (similar to cream cheese) that is a traditional ingredient in tiramisu. Look for it in the specialty cheese section of the supermarket.

1. Preheat oven to 350°F. Line 22 standard (2½-inch) muffin cups with paper baking cups. Stir instant coffee and hot water in medium bowl until coffee is dissolved. Add liqueur; mix well.

2. Beat cake mix, eggs, water and butter in large bowl with electric mixer at medium speed about 3 minutes or until smooth. Remove half of batter to coffee mixture; mix well. Spoon equal amounts of coffee and plain batters into each prepared muffin cup, filling three-fourths full. Swirl batters with toothpick or small paring knife to marbleize.

3. Bake 16 to 18 minutes or until toothpick inserted into centers comes out clean. Cool cupcakes in pans 10 minutes; remove to wire racks to cool completely.

4. Combine mascarpone, powdered sugar and vanilla in medium bowl; mix well. Fold in whipped topping; cover and refrigerate until ready to use.

5. Cut off tops of cupcakes with serrated knife; cut out designs in center of cupcake tops with mini cookie cutters. Spoon filling evenly over cupcake bottoms. Sprinkle cupcake tops with cocoa; place over filling and press down gently. Refrigerate 2 hours before serving.

Makes 22 cupcakes

Double Malted Cupcakes

    2 cups all-purpose flour
    ¼ cup plus 1 tablespoon malted milk powder, divided
    2 teaspoons baking powder
    ¼ teaspoon salt
    1¾ cups granulated sugar
    ¾ cup (1½ sticks) butter, softened, divided
    1 cup milk
    2½ teaspoons vanilla, divided
    3 egg whites
    4 ounces milk chocolate candy bar, broken into chunks
    ¼ cup whipping cream
    1¾ cups powdered sugar
    30 chocolate-covered malt ball candies

1. Preheat oven to 350°F. Line 30 standard (2½-inch) muffin cups with paper baking cups.

2. For cupcakes, combine flour, ¼ cup malted milk powder, baking powder and salt in medium bowl; mix well. Beat granulated sugar and ½ cup butter in large bowl with electric mixer at medium speed 1 minute. Add milk and 1½ teaspoons vanilla; beat at low speed 30 seconds. Gradually beat in flour mixture; beat at medium speed 2 minutes. Add egg whites; beat 1 minute. Spoon batter into prepared muffin cups, filling two-thirds full.

3. Bake 20 minutes or until golden brown and toothpick inserted into centers comes out clean. Cool cupcakes in pans 10 minutes; remove to wire racks to cool completely.

4. For frosting, melt chocolate and remaining ¼ cup butter in heavy medium saucepan over low heat, stirring frequently. Stir in cream, remaining 1 tablespoon malted milk powder and 1 teaspoon vanilla; mix well. Gradually stir in powdered sugar. Cook 4 to 5 minutes, stirring constantly, until lumps disappear. Refrigerate 20 minutes, beating every 5 minutes or until frosting is spreadable. Frost cupcakes; decorate with malt ball candies.

Makes 30 cupcakes

Double Malted Cupcakes

Rocky Road Cupcakes

   1 package (about 18 ounces) chocolate fudge cake mix
1⅓ cups water
  3 eggs
½ cup vegetable oil
¾ cup mini chocolate chips, divided
  1 container (16 ounces) chocolate frosting
  1 cup mini marshmallows
⅔ cup walnut pieces
   Hot fudge ice cream topping or chocolate syrup, heated

1. Preheat oven to 325°F. Line 22 standard (2½-inch) muffin cups with paper baking cups.

2. Beat cake mix, water, eggs, oil and ¼ cup chocolate chips in large bowl with electric mixer at low speed 30 seconds. Beat at medium speed 2 minutes or until well blended. Spoon batter into prepared muffin cups, filling two-thirds full.

3. Bake 20 minutes or until toothpick inserted into centers comes out clean. Cool cupcakes in pans 10 minutes; remove to wire racks to cool completely.

4. Spread thin layer of frosting over cupcakes. Top with marshmallows, walnuts and remaining ½ cup chocolate chips, pressing down lightly to adhere to frosting. Drizzle with hot fudge topping.

Makes 22 cupcakes

Rocky Road Cupcakes

Chocolate Hazelnut Cupcakes

- 1¾ cups all-purpose flour
- 1½ teaspoons baking powder
- ½ teaspoon salt
- 2 cups chocolate hazelnut spread, divided
- ⅓ cup (⅔ stick) butter, softened
- ¾ cup sugar
- 2 eggs
- 1 teaspoon vanilla
- 1¼ cups milk
- Chopped hazelnuts (optional)

1. Preheat oven to 350°F. Line 18 standard (2½-inch) muffin cups with paper or foil baking cups.

2. Combine flour, baking powder and salt in medium bowl. Beat ⅓ cup chocolate hazelnut spread and butter in large bowl with electric mixer at medium speed until smooth. Beat in sugar until well blended. Beat in eggs and vanilla. Add flour mixture alternately with milk, beginning and ending with flour mixture. Spoon batter into prepared muffin cups, filling two-thirds full.

3. Bake 20 to 23 minutes or until toothpick inserted into centers comes out clean. Cool cupcakes in pans 10 minutes; remove to wire racks to cool completely.

4. Frost cupcakes with remaining 1⅔ cups chocolate hazelnut spread. Sprinkle with hazelnuts, if desired.

Makes 18 cupcakes

Chocolate Hazelnut Cupcakes

Classic Chocolate Cupcakes

1¾ cups all-purpose flour

1¼ cups sugar

 2 teaspoons baking powder

½ teaspoon salt

¾ cup vegetable oil

¾ cup milk

 3 eggs

1½ teaspoons vanilla

 8 squares (1 ounce each) semisweet baking chocolate, melted and cooled slightly

   Chocolate Buttercream Frosting (page 126)

   Colored sprinkles (optional)

1. Preheat oven to 350°F. Line 20 standard (2½-inch) muffin cups with paper baking cups.

2. Combine flour, sugar, baking powder and salt in large bowl. Add oil, milk, eggs and vanilla; beat with electric mixer at medium speed 2 minutes or until well blended. Stir in melted chocolate until well blended. Spoon batter into prepared muffin cups, filling three-fourths full.

3. Bake 25 to 30 minutes or until toothpick inserted into centers comes out clean. Cool cupcakes in pans 10 minutes; remove to wire racks to cool completely.

4. Prepare Chocolate Buttercream Frosting; spread over cooled cupcakes. Decorate with sprinkles, if desired. *Makes 20 cupcakes*

Classic Chocolate Cupcakes

Chocolate Buttercream Frosting

    4 cups powdered sugar, sifted, divided
    ¾ cup (1½ sticks) butter, softened
    6 squares (1 ounce each) unsweetened chocolate, melted and cooled slightly
    8 tablespoons milk, divided
    ¾ teaspoon vanilla

1. Beat 2 cups powdered sugar, butter, melted chocolate, 4 tablespoons milk and vanilla in large bowl with electric mixer at medium speed until smooth.

2. Add remaining 2 cups sugar; beat until light and fluffy, adding more milk, 1 tablespoon at a time, if needed to reach desired spreading consistency.

Buttercream Frosting

    1 cup (2 sticks) butter
    1 teaspoon vanilla
    ¼ teaspoon salt
    1 tablespoon meringue powder
    1 tablespoon milk
    1 package (16 ounces) powdered sugar

1. Beat butter, vanilla and salt in medium bowl with electric mixer at medium-high speed until fluffy.

2. Beat in meringue powder and milk. Gradually add powdered sugar until well blended. Beat at high speed 5 minutes or until frosting is light and fluffy. Use immediately or refrigerate up to 1 week. (If refrigerated, bring frosting to room temperature and beat until light and fluffy before using.)

METRIC CONVERSION CHART

VOLUME MEASUREMENTS (dry)

$1/8$ teaspoon = 0.5 mL
$1/4$ teaspoon = 1 mL
$1/2$ teaspoon = 2 mL
$3/4$ teaspoon = 4 mL
1 teaspoon = 5 mL
1 tablespoon = 15 mL
2 tablespoons = 30 mL
$1/4$ cup = 60 mL
$1/3$ cup = 75 mL
$1/2$ cup = 125 mL
$2/3$ cup = 150 mL
$3/4$ cup = 175 mL
1 cup = 250 mL
2 cups = 1 pint = 500 mL
3 cups = 750 mL
4 cups = 1 quart = 1 L

VOLUME MEASUREMENTS (fluid)

1 fluid ounce (2 tablespoons) = 30 mL
4 fluid ounces ($1/2$ cup) = 125 mL
8 fluid ounces (1 cup) = 250 mL
12 fluid ounces ($1 1/2$ cups) = 375 mL
16 fluid ounces (2 cups) = 500 mL

WEIGHTS (mass)

$1/2$ ounce = 15 g
1 ounce = 30 g
3 ounces = 90 g
4 ounces = 120 g
8 ounces = 225 g
10 ounces = 285 g
12 ounces = 360 g
16 ounces = 1 pound = 450 g

DIMENSIONS

$1/16$ inch = 2 mm
$1/8$ inch = 3 mm
$1/4$ inch = 6 mm
$1/2$ inch = 1.5 cm
$3/4$ inch = 2 cm
1 inch = 2.5 cm

OVEN TEMPERATURES

250°F = 120°C
275°F = 140°C
300°F = 150°C
325°F = 160°C
350°F = 180°C
375°F = 190°C
400°F = 200°C
425°F = 220°C
450°F = 230°C

BAKING PAN SIZES

Utensil	Size in Inches/Quarts	Metric Volume	Size in Centimeters
Baking or Cake Pan (square or rectangular)	$8 \times 8 \times 2$	2 L	$20 \times 20 \times 5$
	$9 \times 9 \times 2$	2.5 L	$23 \times 23 \times 5$
	$12 \times 8 \times 2$	3 L	$30 \times 20 \times 5$
	$13 \times 9 \times 2$	3.5 L	$33 \times 23 \times 5$
Loaf Pan	$8 \times 4 \times 3$	1.5 L	$20 \times 10 \times 7$
	$9 \times 5 \times 3$	2 L	$23 \times 13 \times 7$
Round Layer Cake Pan	$8 \times 1 1/2$	1.2 L	20×4
	$9 \times 1 1/2$	1.5 L	23×4
Pie Plate	$8 \times 1 1/4$	750 mL	20×3
	$9 \times 1 1/4$	1 L	23×3
Baking Dish or Casserole	1 quart	1 L	—
	$1 1/2$ quart	1.5 L	—
	2 quart	2 L	—